MIDDAY AT THE SUPER-KAMIOKANDE

MATTHEW TIERNEY

COACH HOUSE BOOKS | TORONTO

first edition

 Canada Council **Conseil des Arts**  ONTARIO ARTS COUNCIL
for the Arts du Canada CONSEIL DES ARTS DE L'ONTARIO
an Ontario government agency
un organisme du gouvernement de l'Ontario Canadä

Published with the generous assistance of the Canada Council for the Arts
and the Ontario Arts Council. Coach House Books also acknowledges the
support of the Government of Canada through the Canada Book Fund
and the Government of Ontario through the Ontario Book Publishing
Tax Credit.

LIBRARY AND ARCHIVES CANADA CATALOGUING IN PUBLICATION

Tierney, Matthew Frederick, 1970-, author
        Midday at the Super-Kamiokande / Matthew Tierney.

Poems.
Issued in print and electronic formats.
ISBN 978-1-55245-377-3 (softcover)

        I. Title.

PS8589.I42M53 2018   C811'.6   C2018-903928-0
                                         C2018-903929-9

Midday at the Super-Kamiokande is available as an ebook: ISBN 978 1
77056 575 3 (EPUB), ISBN 978 1 77056 576 0 (PDF).

Purchase of the print version of this book entitles you to a free digital copy.
To claim your ebook of this title, please email sales@chbooks.com with
proof of purchase. (Coach House Books reserves the right to terminate
the free digital download offer at any time.)

For August

CONTENTS

*Order is always
starting over.*

– Kay Ryan

THE FUTURE OF HUMANITY
SINCE 1945

A warlike alien race has
breached the brane of our star system
like a gas leak in a waiting room.
My doctor says it's all in my head
while pointing to her own.

Tinnitus. *In loco*. There you go.

It's just an accident I
found a copy of *Being and Nothingness*
on an otherwise empty bus.
It's happenstance alone we're alone.

Magic hour in the arcade.
A thin Asian man retro-walks,
quadriceps working against the westerly.
Behind the balustrade I spy on him
for the time left on my watch.

Imagine a point in your life
when you can't imagine it any other way.
That's bliss.
Now switch.
Welcome to the resistance.

CLOSER THAN FAR, FAR AWAY

Into the window flies the swallow.

Twice a year I play the lotto:
on my birthday and the day I'm to die.
Like fat Elvis, a Tuesday.

Woman, O hard-headed woman
walking up the sidewalk with
a full-length acanthus-leaf mirror,
I remember you blowing me a kiss
even if you didn't.

Metaphysics is so hokey. The plot twists!
You put your whole self in.
You turn it all about.

I was a new father
before I finally figured it out:
the bagpiper on the corner was
playing the theme from *Star Wars*.

URSA MINOR WITH THE NAKED EYE

Three green plastic bushes per sill
in the mall promenade.
A poor man's Platonic ideal,
like the subset that forms in my heart
for the Tyrolean girls of retail.

Omniscience reigns over
the subjects that objects divide.
Not to say you aren't lab rats but
I believe you believe I believe in free will.

Under the lodestar, snow.
A beggar holds his cardboard square:
    Inoperable Brain Cancer
    Need $$$
I cry, 'What for?'

It's possible for preceding events
to happen in any order,
so too the following.

Citywide, toddlers are being revived
in unlicenced daycares.
When attacked by a grizzly
you're supposed to lie there, little bear.

1948–

The nuclear family
gathers in the parlour
with an unspoken belief in the art
of the perfect murder.
Mood rings belong

to a *soi-disant* future.
Soybean fields the yellow of serous fluid
beneath elevated Maglev tracks.
God the author is declared
a dead ringer for Isaac Asimov.

The long view is longing.

A see-saw sits
at the base of the drive-in's monolith.
In space no one can get a laugh.
Zero-gravity toilet humour:
    Passengers are advised
    to read instructions before use.

'Aurora, Ontario, Canada, the Earth,
solar system, Milky Way, universe...'

Memory, merely an
evolutionary side effect
of our need to plan for contingencies.
This one of a young wife with child
isn't even mine.

It's now 1969.

SPIN, LITTLE NEUTRAL ONE

You
as nucleon,
as fetus in an ultrasound,
undersized and undone.
As analysand.

'I'm lowly.'

Love inheres.
Love is zero or non-zero.
Love, is it ever dark in there.

Listen closely.
Before you pass through,
hear us, your interlocutors
in outer space.

TWIN TURN

I'm milliseconds behind you.
Ever since my time in orbit,
it's impossible to keep up.

On flyby I see
ice fractures in Lake Baikal
as rifts in the psyche.
On landing I'm made whole.
A criss-cross of freeways draws
my taxi to the shore.

The little of this
that happened to happen
did little to predict how I'd remember it.
Like information loss in a black hole,
like certain faith in the mystery,
a paradox.

The blue I have in mind
suffused the pre-apocalypse.

Floes form a crystal lattice
to the far point of our deepest lake.
Somewhere, its deepest part.

DODECAHEDRON INSIDE A SPHERE

Positive thinking never works.

One eye on the page,
one on the spider crawling over the desk
toward the hairs on my arm.
The third on the negative space
between.

A syzygy? Good question.
At the centre of every sphere,
a pointless dimension.

For Pythagoreans
uneven numbers are 'more perfect,'
which is extraordinarily odd.
Perhaps, per Plotinus, 'One might be
unaware that one has something...'

A few blocks away
the Old City Hall clock strikes
twelve gongs in one go.
Don't ask me how I know what I know
to be noon.

MIDNIGHT IS MIDDAY AT THE SUPER-KAMIOKANDE

Nothing's ungettable.
Sometimes scratching
is purely recreational.

Neighbour, might I point out
your dog's midnight yap sounds like
a plonked key in the upper octaves.
Also: the lemming leading the charge
over the cliff
dies a lemming.

Under Mount Ikeno
they're counting on the WIMP miracle.
Those in the know say
'a thousand thousand years from now'
when they mean a million.

Every sun is a full sun.
Every sun ends as the image of sun
in a field of phones
inclined over the canyon.

Warmth ebbs.
With darkness we unlock the looking,
FWIW.

CRASH COURSE IN COSMOGONY

Weird. Friday to Sunday my
thoughts unwind in alphabetical order.
Monday on, they rewind.

Black black. Blacker
than a stock ticker in October.
The totalled U-Haul, opposite lane,
deployed driver's side airbag
like a used condom
dangled to size up the cum.

I have a recurring dream where
my twin stabs me with a compass.
'The circle jerk is complete,' he seethes,
tragically misreading Nietzsche.

Brute fact: humanism will find a way
to fuck up a surprise party.

Fatal, says CP24's live stream.
John Doe is done,
like gold to airy thinness beat.
This week's unofficial Wheel of Fortune:
BACON BEAR COTTAGE FOREST PINE PUCK.

HOODLESS, HEEDFUL

The mauled pigeon
palpitates on the sidewalk,
its fate as useless as art.
Little consolation to those of us

given to fits of consultation.
You learn your soft parts
the hard way, coos Lady Philosophy.
Let he who spooked the bird of prey
on the creature's breast
make no mistake with his heel.

Me?
    You.

Having someone with whom
to share your weird, wired dream
is one win short of win-win.

What dark clouds had obscured
blazes forth between each shade tree.
     STEEL
     PLATE
     AHEAD
is a reflective equilateral road sign
I've just read.

A BLUNT INSTRUMENT MAKES ITS OWN SWEET KIND OF MUSIC

On the run from sin?
Find yourself a sleepy hollow
and finally start that novel, like me.
I'm writing a supernatural whodunit,
some of it set hereabouts,
some in the hereafter.

My better angel, he turns out to be
a psycho harpist.

I open with Duns Scotus
taking the crosstown nimbus
as a silver-faced mime with top hat.
Passengers feign disinterest
in the myriad mirrors
affixed to his stiffened sport jacket.

Therein
lies the *mise en scène*.

When establishing your MO
choose happiness over the good.
Dirty realism concedes
character is lossy, not Hi-Fi.

The everlasting fractures.
The harp ships ACTUAL SIZE.

RED STATE BLUE

Burkas every Monday
shoulder to shoulder on the clothesline,
a swaying chorus line.

There's a bursting in air.
I imagine Francis Scott Key
nose down in a Floridian puddle.
My father, after we fled to Canada,
whistled round the clock that Buffet song –
don't you, don't you *dare*.

To a psychoacoustician
mantras are enchantments,
and the sound of a metal sheet, when shaken,
helps sell to Charlton Heston
the Lord's commandment.

Christ. The Easter of my youth
entombed with a twenty-one-gun salute.

Thunder real close.
Up and down our suburban street,
car alarms go off: a flock headed south
toward an American dream.

NEVER NEVERMORE

In the quad the dorky couple
poses for engagement photos for a photog
who's like a headache performing a handjob.
'Don't keep it to yourself!' she shrieks,
meaning love.

In another five billion years
she'll permanently lose her sun
and, with it, the last good argument for
a denim purse with rainbow sequins.

You defeat the purpose
if you practice for a three-legged race

and win.
'Better to burn out, any day,'
my wife's forever saying.
She stitches proverbs onto throw pillows.
She's an original.

We're back at day's end
drying dishes around sunset.
'Nothing rhymes with orange,' I insist.
'No it doesn't,' she sighs, never more distant.

ROUTINE MAINTENANCE MISSION

My wife loves me.
Still I'm not certain I'm not
a sleeper agent awaiting a trigger.
Like a Cartesian doing stand-up
I've entertained the thought.

Ancient history is full of
unenlightened spacemen
who take autopilot for granted.
By 'ancient history,' I mean the fifties.
By 'fifties,' I mean the golden age of sci-fi.

My subway stop has been
under construction for three seasons,
the chief machine a red behemoth
with the designation EARTH BORING 4.

Again the morning paper refers to
'enhanced interrogation techniques.'
I think *anal probe*, not *waterboard*.
Just minding my p's and q's,

looking forward to French Toast Friday
with real maple syrup,
when my wife momentarily flickers.
Her true alien self in a rose-pink bathrobe.

POEM WITH NO MIDDLE

Begin with Anaxagoras:
'Appearances are a glimpse of the obscure.'
End with the painbirds of Mark Linkous
as Sparklehorse.

Begin earlier in the day.
That tote printed with Klimt's *The Kiss*
bouncing through the crosswalk, east to my west,
Nouveau to Deco to décor to art
to King Arthur cuckolded by Sir Lancelot –
if you follow.

The hum I'll never hear
has been with me since birth.
The truth, it bursts

and disperses aporia.
I prefer 'sarsaparilla' to root beer.
I pair 'preplanning' with 'funeral';
needless to point out, I pin ribbons with
needles to point out.

It's late.
At the end of the hall,
unearthly yellow under the door
underscores who's awake.

ZOON LOGON ECHON

Scientists agree
the world's running out of fun facts.
Even if you can't read the signs

from where you're standing,
as a rational animal you accept
the ultimate Playground Rule:
　　　Think before you act.

An Ornge helicopter
vectors into the blue.

'To become human
does not come easily'; to stay human
click on the drawing room lamp.
Light, child, keeps at bay the howling
albino zombie mob.

O lord of the infernal engines!
In the user manual, *explode grenade*
has through generation loss
devolved into *exploit agenda*
and goosed our extinction rate.

The last of the pterosaurs
thumps rhythmically against
its iron cage.

ECSTATIC TEMPORALITY
FOR DUMMIES

Hat brims, lapel pins, taupe vests.
The class of portrait photographers
with vintage cameras
hops around me, my pint, the patio.
A single robin settles on a point of view.

Idealists ask grandiose questions.
Realists spring a pop quiz.
Like, when stranded on a desert island,
with what material and to what scale
should one spell out HELP?

Seconds, days, years,
we feel them pass psychologically.
Brain scientists can now use
reverse psychology
to transport you to the Roaring Twenties,
the Left Bank, Boulevard Saint-Germain –

Probably not your idea of a good time.
Forget I said anything.

A ladybug plays dead on
the coast of my dampened coaster.
A plane burbles above my big wobbly head.

WEE REIGN

My Coca-Cola core, decarbonated.

The lunch hour is faulty.
I hover on the path's asphalt
reading then rereading
the red spray paint on it:
>   *We're*
>   *coming*
>   *for you,*
>   BRB.

This gold glitter in my hair.
A necessary truth is *in here*.
Out there the aliens arrive
and vapourize SETI first thing
for some bloody peace and quiet already.

We call it the Very Large Array
because it's very large and very very.
We call it 'the same cough'
not for its duration, volume, or timbre
but its microscopic source.

Dear denizens of
multipurpose green space,
please believe me when I say
whichever direction I face, that's north.

THE DERELICT OF DEERLICK CREEK

Under garden wreaths
dry-cleaning hangs from door knockers
of multimillion-dollar homes.

A life of true belief
needs no justification.
Stand behind any window in
my many-roomed dream house
and your gaze falls on flat earth.

Two, maybe three, cardinals
alternate summer-long as phenomena
within the property-line thicket.
Every year the same two,

maybe three, I see no alternative.
Pure reason has let me alone
to click beads like antinomies.

An etched R SECRET PACT
in the retaining wall's feathered concrete.
I love my Stockholm syndrome.
I think the world of it.

UPPER LOWER MIDDLE

At Starbucks all is normal.
Caramel flan latte.
Breakfast-wrap eggs laid in
behavioural-enriched colony housing
somewhere not *too* too local.

The future is as it always was,
the keys to the washroom
moored to shoehorns.

Working alone, a solipsist solves
the hard problem of consciousness;
nobody is impressed.
A physicist discovers a theory of everything
that fails to explain nothing.

You can spot neurotypicals
by our displays of affection,
the dandelion glow under our chins.
Surfing the noosphere on Kickstarter,
one argument from design
to another.

We practice *realpolitik*,
carve out space for ourselves
in the abyss.

ZIGGURAT ZAG

It's thirty degrees
and feels like thirty – that never happens.
Far down the sidewalk in the heat,
a superfluity of nuns
stands its ground.

Yesterday is figured out.
Yesterday is Archimedes
scratching diagrams in the dust.
Today's the invading Roman soldier
who brained him *in medias res.*

Last night was an honour,
to play a small part in 'the most
comprehensive consumer safety recall
in American history.'

Habits click in place
like black patio umbrellas.
For a year our local Dollarama
has stacked its window-display stock
like a Sumerian tower:
  Empty Tin Boxes, $3

Tomorrow I'll ask the storekeeper
how much for just the tin.

SIGNAL TO NOISE

Pig snouts, pig ears
poke through the panels of the transport,
a spectre panning past us.
Oh the squealing,
as if arranged by Phil Spector.

(You will remember. You will.)

Nullity: a spherical
spacetime of radius zero.
Nothing equals emptiness, while nothingness
emptiness when thought full...
I'm tired of

talking through the door.
So many fictions chronicled, ingrown.
'Truth is subjectivity,' said L. Ron.
'Freedom's for honest people,' said Søren.

One liar is not like the other.
The other liar is not me.

A body snatcher
makes the mouth sounds of
Thomas Cruise Mapother IV
accepting his Freedom Medal of Valor.
Can you hear him – you can hear him –
disavow our psychic overlords
over and over, happily ever after.

LONGTIME LISTENER

Our Lady of Perpetual Help
has new storefront signage;
prayer requests are 'by appointment only.'
Only an atheist would comment on
the medieval font.

The point at which
a passing car's hubcaps
seem to stall then revolve backwards,
that's when you fall half in love.
The tunnel light a stainless steel

known to stain in rare cases.
Like the DJ therapists with the suicide pact.
Envision them together, weightless
in the Large Magellanic Cloud, 'exit bags'
sempiternally attached,
ballooned with hydrogen gas.

In any argument from a premise,
the last word is true or false.

INBREAKING

At heart a Jewish rationalist, just
diagnosed with fear and trembling –
is it possible to conceive of
not death
but never having existed?

A show of hands, everyone, for 'yes.'

Note my spirited approach.
Near the far end of Ghost Ranch,
the glass church throws back an image
of a shadow self, mushrooming.
Behind me desert beryl, the odd
successful cloud.

A newborn nightmare
flares methane blue.
My hands cup the pane.
Row on row of congregant faces
face an outside with me inside.

WHO SAYS OWL THE OWL WHO SAYS WHO

The riddle that doesn't rhyme
doesn't exist, said Wittgenstein.
No word of a lie is to blame.

1 of the most deceptive books ever.
The Boy Who Came Back from Heaven
brought us down to earth,
a status update
he had to type with his mouth.

On the playscape, snow buildup
tumbles like rabbits; quivers, stops.
Existence precedes entrance
into the day-bright necropolis…
the wandering prince is trapped!

Riddlemaster,
here's another game: my son
hands me the Winnie-the-Pooh puppet
so he can talk directly to it.

Who's playing who? Now I ask you.

GLINDA THE GOOD IS GONE

A crosswind – the Norway's leaves flash
like sunfish in a man-made pond.
Still waiting for someone to ask
if I believe in God.

Maple keys footnote the ground.
As a metaphor maker I'm qualified
to point out the asterisks.

A quantum resonance
separates the perfect day
from the perfect day for a funeral.
A question of which question, which universe,

witch principal.
I pray the priest at her deathbed
took a moment, fluffed the pillows.

Weeks later two cawing crows flush
a hawk from the now-bare tree
with a fear unlike fear.

Because because because because because.

INTERA

MISSION

JUPITER AND BEYOND

Away from all suns?
    – Nietzsche

1

Heaven is timeless;
therefore, no music.
New arrivals file in, surprised by this.

Would you believe a
blown semi-trailer retread
in curls on the gravel shoulder
prods me into a leap of – ?

Maybe faith is *causa sui.*
Or a string of conditionals like
switchbacks on the road to Mesa Verde.
Or the iffy moment when
not-so-distant sheet lightning
flashes over the Bruce Peninsula.

Maybe He works the way
left-handed scissors refuse to work
in your right.

2

May, and the sawed-off branch
on our mulberry tree
has dripped water all spring,
discolouring a single hexagonal
interlocking stone.

In July, the Juno spacecraft
emits the tone for burn cutoff,
shifts telemetry,
and enters Jupiter's orbit.

Fruitless February.
Lobsters at Loblaws
claw toward the pump's froth.

September, remembering
last month, when your bedroom blinds
picked up the rhythm of the wind
then set it down.

Thus: August.

3

His voice through speakers.
Staticky for the responsorial psalm,
shorting out by the homily.
Turning the mic off
sounds radical.

'Can you hear me in the back?
Good.'

It took me
decades to feel God's absence,
mere seconds to infer
a presence;

as though
I answered a HELP WANTED sign
in a secondhand store
and found the sign itself for sale.

4

An irruption of logic.
Is loss *ekstasis*?

5

Rip-aimed like little tears.
Asked 'Why are you screaming?'
the purist answers with more scream.
In one respect
having a bad dream's the same

as watching an aurora in a magstorm.
You promptly forget the conditions
necessary and sufficient
for its existence.

The programmed drive to the surface.
Juno's titanium vault holds
a Lego Galileo, in honour of.

In the Renaissance room. Its end song.

6

In Doppler residuals
the ephemeral lives on.

Thus the singular is ours.

Thus
when you're not with me:
hidden just enough to be seen,
bracketed by the reeds, the frog
you would love so
so much.

A FISHERMAN FISHES FOR FISH

Dents in the storm clouds
as though beaten with a ball-peen hammer.
The last thought I remember –
lightning's far more likely
to strike metaphorically.

The closest I got to Jesus
was that day at the post office.
A lifetime ago.

Pontius Pilate owns the cameo,
Michelangelo the Hitchcock zoom.
What have I lent my name to?
What will I take to my grave?
What scholar would ever exclaim, 'Him
I'd love to exhume!'

They finally fall, the rains,
a bloom of pearly, pearly blue.

COMEDOWN WITH COMEUPPANCE

Everything is identical to itself
except the duck-billed platypus.
Nothing is the same.

BREAKING:
Landslide in Mumbai, Hundreds Dead.
Not a flood but 'a flood event,'
the same phrase the plumber used
for the sewage in my basement.

Just so happens neither of us
believes in coincidence.

The carefree me
wears a tinfoil hat whose mod design
jams my place cells from firing.
Now where was I?

Off the new cedar deck a
spider web from leaf to railing
reads as optical fibre in twilit purple.
Evolution sure can be beautiful.
That moment of freefall

when you miss the last stair,
realizing the lie is not possible.

BOY GENIUS

An old valentine, my Alison, in the dailies.

Years ago, when the condom broke,
I flashed to a future where
I shamble the length of a subway car
to avoid her.

You're thinking once.
You're half right.

Kant hits upon the transcendental realm
one incandescent afternoon
by focusing on a floater in his eye.
Einstein, on walks at Princeton,
briefly notices how his shadow falls
faster than the speed of light.

My gut tells me
hindsight is just a hunch
in reverse.

Doors open to an off-world.
In I step: young, brainy, to the nines
as Ensign Wesley Crusher.

CRUSHER

This might sound strange, mister,
but *you're* the problem. Not me.

TIERNEY

You're right, Wes.
(a beat)
That does sound strange.

THE AIR IN
QUOTE–UNQUOTE SCARE

Don't I know
a pocket square can be misplaced,
pinstripes the wrong colour –
if Tungsten Angst is even a colour.

Three Halloweens in a row
I went as the life of the party.
At home I've got every light on timer.
Twice a day the lampshades sing hosanna
and then don't I know

to feed my bearded dragon.
'Believe it!' the milk carton says again,
'Cancer will be conquered in our lifetime.'

At my high school reunion
don't I suspect I'm not
the smartest guy in the room, in leather pants,
but the smartest guy in the room in leather pants.

Beware the personal salutation.
Beware the air quotes, the pen click
as the doc frowns at your chart.

Down the street, in the dark,
my house lit up like a close encounter.

FLUTE SOLO IN ZERO-G

In my dream within a dream,
I betrayed myself as
leader of the robot revolution
by saying everything twice.
Then I woke up; then I woke up.

I must be the only human
who couldn't pass the Turing test
in his sleep.

Is NO PULP a reasonable demand?
'The happier I get, the sadder I am' –
this from my heuristic algorithms
after a slow morning wank.

Mars rises in the porthole like a red cent.
Its truth-value, at long last, greenlit.
At the denotative moment

the morning star has the good sense
to put in an appearance as Venus.
Later the evening goddess
lays my doubts to rest.

EVERYTHING HAPPENS TO ME

A billboard on the off-ramp:
> *Thinking about suicide?*
> *We can help.*

It's been explained to me
more times than I can count
how one infinity can be larger than another.
A mnemonic toll-free number
is a small mercy.

Ontologically speaking,
it's impossible to be better than you are,
only better than you were
when you Googled, half curious,
'homemade lethal cocktail.'

I perfectly recall
making out on her parents' divan.
I am young and purposeful.
Around the corner in the kitchen,
they play crokinole, stoned on rye 'n' Cokes
and 'Bad Moon Rising.'

What happens next is real.

In every universe ending in zero,
drop a turtle on a turntable
and it crawls into the spin.

THE CANARY SINGS OXEN FREE

They put a keypad on a wristwatch
and I knew what it was to be a man.
So many buttonholes in '81

for the Stasi to hide a camera in.
I miss DIY fashion, analogue hiss,
our surprise when we learned we
had come through the title sequence.

It's true,
staying awake on a long drive
is like wrestling a giant octopus.
What choice is there for an optimist.
Nothing good happens in
an underground garage.

When she wears the yellow dress,
she's a source of happiness.

Oh the satellite clear of the storm
blinks off and on –
three long, three long, three long.
To find middle C close your eyes
and walk into the tall pines.
Count backward from a million to one.

PROJECTS MANHATTAN TO PARSONS, ALAN

The so-called universal tour
needs more waterfall, less barrel.

Like a Bohr electron a baby squirrel
plummets from branch to ground –
thunk. Thunk,
a tick on the Doomsday Clock.

A boy tents in his own yard,
marshals foot soldiers in a toy army.
From the back gate, an interrobang.
From the bay doors, an atom bomb.

The red dawn sky changes chords.
You may have a private word
for the pain of phenomena.
Whatever you think it means,
it is out of the ordinary.

Mama squirrel jitterbugs over the corpse.
All grief plays as parody
from the sniper's nest.

OPPENHEIMER'S SOUL AND THE MATHEMATICAL SUBLIME

The man with a tattoo of
da Vinci's *The Last Supper*
the entire length of his forearm
reveals something about belief or beauty.
It's for us to choose.

Down the gallery hall
a Baroque sculpture of Christ crucified,
suffering as normal.
Life-sized.

How far are you willing to go?

1951, Nevada.
Fur afire from the blast wave,
a rabbit lights out over the desert floor
outrunning recurring terror.
Here's as close to

the truth as I can get you:
radiation from a tube TV
could separate the human form
from matter.

If you think you can imagine that,
you possibly can't.

DEFCON 4

The telephone cord
induced the very pacing it restrained.
When Terry Fox dipped his prosthetic
into the chilly Atlantic,
cancer was along for the run.

Idling thirty years on
in highway traffic, a marathon of inches.
Electronic PSA, sign of the modern:
    That text or call could end it all.

Southbound, a drumroll.
Existential dread

never shows in a photo.
Who would guess our avenues
both contained and contained the threat
of thermonuclear war.

Life's incurable, with intervals of relief.
We are and remain aware
and undescended.

FADED JADE

Envy is
an invasive Irish ivy.

Momentarily in love,
my nucleus accumbens lights up.
To a philosopher, the truth maker.
To a scientist, the proof to be disproved.
To the technician, a spark plug.

Cosmic microwaves strike my skin.
'We have our limits,' said Kant,
who had no way of foreseeing Usain Bolt
or – horror! –
what's in the thing itself is people.

The radiologist
drapes a lead apron over my vitals.
Look, its shape and colour
resemble the sea inside Bikini Atoll.
Here I lie! Under the thumb of Apollo!

Nothing much impresses her
and I don't understand why
that impresses me so much.

BOTH NEITHER AND NOR

'A Manichean would say
there are two kinds of Manicheans:
practicing and non-practicing.'
So quips the Wikipidean.

Along the roofline a
row of chimney columns
flush to the noon-hour monochrome.
Thin white smoke, like laughter, uncoiling…

Wanted Wednesdays is mugshot heaven.
I click on the Police Services site
and lock eyes with the apophatic,
see the good in every one.

Supersymmetry predicts
for each God particle we observe,
a non-believer has a vision.
Adherents everywhere cling fast

as beings everywhere achieve mass.
Off asphalt, high summer haze
summons my counterpart,
a shimmer in the middlemost.

GLITTER NEAR THE TANNHÄUSER GATE

I've seen things you people
wouldn't believe.

A newish fountain memorial.
The 'eternal flame' oftentimes unlit,
a washed-out wished-for symbol.
Like the silver coin I fish from
the black-tiled pool.

Since you ask,
being present feels like
sitting for the Voight-Kampff.
A pleasant turn through a home movie
with the sound off.

Skin-jobs of a sort,
I look up at dusk, she looks, they look.
The office tower's west face, slick.
Every night we happy ones
whimper in our sleep.

Immortality is not
too much to hope for.
I've seen Rutger Hauer die in the rain
how many times.

YELLOW SUNNY DISPOSITION

In a continuous loop before
the community message board,
trying to guess
which notice went up second:
Band Needs Singer ASAP or
SINGER SEEKS BAND

Wait. Give me a minute.

My infant son with the golden skin
laughs at a fake sneeze, cries at a real one.
A worldview caught between
Patch Adams and Schopenhauer.

My infant son, says El Dorado.
My infant son, says Jor-El.

From the multicoloured pack
choose the red tack to signify
Suffering is Knowledge of the Will.
From the star nearby, light to see by,
as the steel sinks into cork

like a point well made.
There's little you can't forgive.

HOST OF THE INVISIBLE BEHOLDEN

The self-closing-hinge door
at Dark Horse Espresso
resists the force of the wind
and hovers however long.

I admire equally
the counterweight, the equipoise.
A vitreous wing learning its purpose.

How my son bloodied his nose:
he leapt off the bed while
I stood in the wall mirror
reflecting on myself as father figure.

I once read someone
who'd read someone who'd heard someone
say the telephone was invented
to commune with ghosts.

There's no nowhere,
so you have to sit somewhere.
I prefer a view of the exit, who doesn't.

RETROGRADE ARC

for Erik Rutherford

Like a bottomless cup, my head,
always full yet impossible to fill.
Dark and early Sunday morning

I set about drawing a perfect circle.
For a material being, unthinkable.
Come daybreak I find a loophole.

In a past life I was a plant
though how could I know that.

Mondays, the co-op basement,
in a ring around our group leader.
He kicks off as he always kicks off
the imperishable night:
    'If you're here
    for the first time, welcome again.'

I'm self-conscious. You are too.
We can only surprise ourselves
in a roundabout way.

Can you see it? The columns,
the pediments on the mountain.
The temples, fountains, theatre.
Midsummer, domed like thought itself.

VALENCE

The seagull above the shoreline
makes no headway in the wind.
It appears comfortable
as a placeholder.

110% Guarantee
to help with any Evil Affection!
The sandwich board, medium of choice
for mediums everywhere.

Earlier,
vigilance was my watchword.
Your pink blouse and how the afternoon
leapt through the cottage window.
Our son, drawn into your orbit.
One might say he was adopted.

Nature is only good, says Augustine.
Between degrees of goodness, only pain.

The cloud cover moves so slowly
the movement is the clouds.
Behind them, the sun
un-invisible, almost immaterial,
understood by the things that are made.

SEROTONIN BAY

Tube man never flags.
Good times and bad,
he straightens, he bows before
limited offers on hot tubs, spas, saunas.
You say pink, I say what you'd call salmon.

Everywhere I look I get an eyeful.

A woman on the TTC
thumbs open her prayer book:
For Persons with Chemical Dependencies.
A man slips an object of sentiment
into his breast pocket
to guard against a stray bullet.

Under the streetlight, trapped inside
the Flight Centre storefront display,
a red admiral
flutters between getaway deals:
London, Brisbane, Fort Lauderdale.

I couldn't tell you where
can't be gotten to from here.

It takes some searching to find him.
Behind skids of sod, Michael
in a Home Depot apron
practices kendo with a border spade.
There are so many ways to be wrong
that feel right.

THE GOLDILOCKS ZONE

When the thunder shower arrives,
the heavy air around me (how revolutionary)
rises up to meet it.
You'd know the feeling
sheltered in the thick of it.

I'm intrapsychic.
Shortly I'll be gifted
with an ability to foretell the future.
Until then all I remember

has been present perfect.
His tantrum in the bathtub
made possible by the plumbing of
the sufficiently advanced.

Rain soaks
the belongings of an evicted tenant
strewn on the lawn across the street.
A life blown up like some, um,
celestial event.

They should have sent a poet's poet.

Out my cockpit's cockpit,
universal decoherence. Rowhouses.
The key to exiting the wormhole is
don't think about a key.

PEOPLE PLAN

So little room on the platform,
it's dystopian.

Can't decipher whether
my fellow commuter, intent on his tablet,
is a proficient first-person shooter,
if I'm his equal.

Is there any measure more biblical
than a stone's throw?

Underground,
what sunlight there is is refused us.
I've mixed feelings pointing out the obvious.
Either you understand my ambivalence

or you do not.
In the kingdom of conspiracies,
anyone could be a theorist.

On the surface,
fruit rots in horn-shaped bowls.
Mirror man, our hair's turning silver,
last chance to exchange looks.
You first.

MEMORABILITY AS A
CITY OF IMAGES

The deformed, overturned pylon
refinds function
as pillow for the sleeping man.
Content is modular, contentment
an economy of scale.

A massacre of concrete.
Brutalism, by Le Corbusier.

Seated next to the tank
at the local establishment,
I turn away for a moment, turn back.
The goldfish, all facing the same way!

Given enough time
the concert hall synchronizes
its applause,
the pathway goes on

and goes on home.
A blind panhandler has found
an extant pay phone in the core.
Squinting, the receiver to his ear
for an extended period, as though listening.
But clearly just standing there, listening.

EDGE OF THE OBSERVABLE

A young doctor racewalks
through the rotunda, pinned to her phone.
'Blah blah blah blah blah,' she says.

The mornings play out
in Sunnybrook's food court.
I observe carrot-muffin man break off
another mouthful, weigh it in his hand.
Normal matter, dark matters.

Monday, the day of his birth,
my nihilistic chatter – gone.
On the TV overhead, a press conference:
    'We can neither confirm nor deny
    the existence or non-existence
    of an active investigation.'

A master of the black arts, the
commander-in-chief's chief adversary.

I-don't-know-who
paced out PEACE + LOVE
in the spring snow on the parking lot.
That won't last. Nevertheless.
Freed from the desire to fly, I flew.

FLYING OVER AN IMAGINARY PLAIN

Cries mount the a.m., it dawns on me –
that gull is quite far inland.
My escape from REM
like crawling out of a Devonian sea.

Finally I've
come to terms with the infinite.
See, the first thing you grasp is the last.
'That then which nothing greater
can be conceived.'

Nocturnal emission. On my PJS.
It goes without saying.
Leaflets stuff the mailbox:
    Life is full of regrets.
    Replacing your windows shouldn't be.

In the hallway by the Court of Appeals,
drenched in A/C on a button-tuft bench,
I'm the drifter rousted from sleep.
I'm the security guard doing justice to
just doing her job.

One act followed by another.
The day dematerializes,
a zebra in the herd.

NOTES, ERRORS, AND FUN FACTS

The opening epigraph is from Kay Ryan's poem 'Odd Blocks' in *The Best of It.*

p. 14, '1948–': The italicized line is from *2001: A Space Odyssey.*

p. 17, 'Twin Turn': A person in orbit experiences relative velocity time dilation and ages more slowly than a person on the ground. In the seventies, Hawking believed that when a black hole evaporates, it destroys quantum information, which violates physical law.

p. 18, 'Dodecahedron inside a Sphere': Plato ascribed to each of the classical four elements a perfect shape. The fifth element, he said, was represented by the dodecahedron. The full quote from Plotinus reads: 'One might be unaware that one has something, holding onto it more powerfully than if one did know.'

p. 19, 'Midnight Is Midday at the Super-Kamiokande': It is a myth that lemmings commit mass suicide by throwing themselves off cliffs. WIMPs are 'Weakly Interacting Massive Particles.' The WIMP miracle is that they're good candidates for dark matter, which makes up a large percentage of the universe and yet remains invisible.

p. 20, 'Crash Course in Cosmogony': In science and philosophy, a 'brute fact' is one that will never have an explanation. The third line of the last stanza is from John Donne.

p. 21, 'Hoodless, Heedful': The first line of the last stanza is adapted from a line in Boethius's *The Consolations of Philosophy.*

p. 27, 'Zoon Logon Echon': Often translated as 'rational animal,' *zoon logon echon* is attributed to Aristotle by Heidegger with a bogus citation; there is no record of Aristotle using that specific phrase. The quote that begins the fourth stanza is from Kierkegaard. The first line of the penultimate stanza is from the movie *Omega Man.*

p. 28, 'Ecstatic Temporality for Dummies': 'Ecstatic temporality' is from Heidegger and refers to the nexus of past, present, and future that makes up his concept of *Dasein*, or 'Being-in-the-world.'

p. 32, 'Ziggurat Zag': One story has Archimedes dying because he was too absorbed in his dust diagram to give his name to a Roman soldier. The army had been given orders to spare his life.

p. 33, 'Signal to Noise': The cosmologist Alexander Vilenkin originated a scientific definition of nothingness as 'a closed spherical spacetime of zero radius.' The attribution for the two quotes in stanza four has been reversed. Tom Cruise's medal was awarded by the Church of Scientology, as seen in the documentary *Going Clear: Scientology and the Prison of Belief.*

p.34, 'Longtime Listener': It's been theorized that the perceptual phenomenon of a wheel spontaneously rotating in the opposite direction is a mistake the brain makes when interpreting ambiguous visual cues.

p. 36, 'Who Says Owl the Owl Who Says Who': In Wittgenstein's *Tractatus Logico-Philosophicus*, section 6.5 reads: 'The riddle does not exist.' Years after the publication of his bestselling memoir, Alex Malarkey confessed that he did not come back from heaven. He is paralyzed below the neck.

pp. 40–45, 'Jupiter and Beyond': The final title card in *2001: A Space Odyssey* reads 'Jupiter and Beyond the Infinite.' The epigraph is from Nietzsche's *The Gay Science*. The detail of the Help Wanted sign at the end of the third section is borrowed from Kierkegaard. The final scenes of *2001* take place in what commentators refer to as the 'Renaissance room.'

p. 47, 'Comedown with Comeuppance': The law of identity, expressed here as 'everything is identical to itself,' is the first of the three classical laws of thought.

pp. 48–49, 'Boy Genius': Nothing is faster than the speed of light. But if you define a shadow as the boundary between light and dark, then the speed of the boundary has no limits; it's merely a pattern one notices, not a thing.

p. 51, 'Flute Solo in Zero-G': Frege, a founder of modern logic, uses the example of Venus to illustrate the difference between his concepts of sense and denotation. (Venus can be both 'the evening star' and 'the morning star.')

p. 52, 'Everything Happens to Me': The real-world poster copy was amended weeks later to 'Thinking about suicide? There is help.'

p. 55, 'Oppenheimer's Soul and the Mathematical Sublime': Kant's mathematical sublime is the feeling engendered by the superiority of reason over imagination, i.e., our ability to comprehend the magnitude of something we can't grasp with our senses.

p. 58, 'Both Neither and Nor': Supersymmetry hypothesizes that each particle in the Standard Model is paired with another, thus helping to determine the mass of the Higgs boson, the 'God particle.'

p. 59, 'Glitter near the Tannhäuser Gate': The title and italicized lines are from *Blade Runner*.

p. 60, 'Yellow Sunny Disposition': Schopenhauer placed the will at the core of his philosophy; the will can never be satisfied, and this gives rise to his famous pessimism.

p. 63, 'Valence': For Augustine, evil is merely an absence of good. The last line is from Romans 1:20.

p. 66, 'The Goldilocks Zone': A planet is considered to be in the Goldilocks Zone if it's habitable for life. The sci-fi writer Arthur C. Clarke famously said, 'Any sufficiently advanced technology is indistinguishable from magic.' Jodie Foster's character in *Contact* enters a wormhole and witnesses 'some celestial event.' She goes on to say, 'No words to describe it. Poetry! They should have sent a poet.' Decoherence is a theory that explains how the classical world arises from quantum mechanics.

p. 68, 'Memorability as a City of Images': The title comes from the Banham essay that christened Brutalism; he described one of its key aspects as 'Memorability as an Image.' Later, Le Corbusier said the movement began in part because he was presented with 'such a massacre of concrete' to build the Unité d'habitation.

p. 70, 'Flying over an Imaginary Plain': The quote in the second stanza is from Saint Anselm's ontological proof for God's existence. It is hypothesized that the stripes of the zebra make it more difficult for predators to pick out a single animal from the herd.

ACKNOWLEDGEMENTS

To the editors of the magazines and journals where poems first appeared: *The Walrus*: 'People Plan,' 'Glinda the Good Is Gone'; *NewPoetry*: 'Ecstatic Temporality for Dummies,' 'Crash Course in Cosmogony,' 'The Air in Quote–Unquote Scare'; *Juniper*: 'Upper Lower Middle,' 'Oppenheimer's Soul and the Mathematical Sublime,' 'Spin, Little Neutral One'; *The Fiddlehead*: 'The Future of Humanity since 1945,' 'The Canary Sings Oxen Free'; *The Malahat Review*: 'Both Neither and Nor,' 'Comedown with Comeuppance,' 'The Derelict of Deerlick Creek'; *The Puritan*: 'Closer Than Far, Far Away'; *Arc Poetry Review*: 'Flute Solo in Zero-G,' 'Routine Maintenance Mission'; *Riddle Fence*: 'Everything Happens to Me,' 'Projects Manhattan to Parsons, Alan,' 'Never Nevermore,' 'Wee Reign'; *Hazlitt*: 'Ursa Minor with the Naked Eye'; and *Lemonhound*: 'Longtime Listener': Thank you.

To the Canada Council for the Arts and the Ontario Arts Council, for providing financial assistance; to Alana Wilcox and the Coach House team, for their unwavering support; to Kevin Connolly and Steve McOrmond, for their candour and percipience as early readers; to Karen Solie, for her intelligence, patience, and persistence in shaping this book: Thank you.

To my wife, Charmaine, and my son, August, for everything else: Love you.

Matthew Tierney is the author of three previous collections of poetry: *Full Speed through the Morning Dark*, *The Hayflick Limit*, and *Probably Inevitable*. He has received the Trillium Book Award for Poetry, the P. K. Page Founders' Award, and the K. M. Hunter Artists' Award. He lives in Toronto.

Typeset in Warnock and Aviano Sans

Printed at the Coach House on bpNichol Lane in Toronto, Ontario, on Zephyr Antique Laid paper, which was manufactured, acid-free, in Saint-Jérôme, Quebec, from second-growth forests. This book was printed with vegetable-based ink on a 1973 Heidelberg KORD offset litho press. Its pages were folded on a Baumfolder, gathered by hand, bound on a Sulby Auto-Minabinda, and trimmed on a Polar single-knife cutter.

Edited for the press by Karen Solie
Designed by Alana Wilcox
Cover image by Cristiana Couceiro
Author photo by Phil Brown

Coach House Books
80 bpNichol Lane
Toronto ON M5S 3J4
Canada

416 979 2217
800 367 6360

mail@chbooks.com
www.chbooks.com